The LADY of the LAKE

Lake Crescent

By Mavis Amundson

**Western Gull Publishing,
a division of the
Peninsula Daily News**

**Western Gull Publishing,
a division of the
Peninsula Daily News
305 W. First St.
Port Angeles, WA 98362**

ISBN 0-9610910-6-1

Cover photograph by Rich Riski, Port Angeles, WA
Inset photo of Hallie Latham Illingworth reproduced by
Ed Hosselkus, Port Angeles, WA
Cover design by Jennifer O'Brien, Seattle, WA

Alexander Printing Company, Inc., Everett, WA

The Lady of the Lake

On a warm July afternoon in 1940, two trout fishermen spotted a body floating on the surface of Lake Crescent in Washington State's Olympic National Park. It was the body of a woman, wearing a wool dress, underwear and silk stockings that were rolled with garters above the knees. The woman was hog-tied with heavy rope and wrapped in blankets. She had been strangled.

Even more macabre was the condition of the body. The woman's face was unrecognizable, but her body had not decomposed. In a bizarre chemical transformation, the flesh had "saponified"— turned into a soap-like substance that could be scooped away like putty. The public's imagination was caught by the grisly discovery, and the murdered woman became known as the "Lady of the Lake." It was a fitting appellation for a mystery woman who had emerged from the cold, deep lake that had a reputation for never giving up its dead.

The body was taken away for examination. Over time, the curious and the concerned came to look at the murdered woman, but no one knew her. After two months she was buried in the county cemetery.

More than a year passed before investigators identified the body as the remains of Hallie Illingworth, a once-beautiful waitress who was last seen a few days before Christmas in 1937 in Port Angeles, a small mill town west of Seattle and about 15 miles from Lake Crescent. Her identification led to a sensational murder trial in 1942 that drew widespread interest in the Northwest. Media coverage of the trial sometimes eclipsed news of World War II in regional newspapers.

In a strange twist of fate, the lake that had been Hallie's crypt for so long had also been her greatest ally. The cold, clean waters of Lake Crescent had preserved her body for an uncommon time — thereby preserving the evidence needed to bring her killer to justice. It was as though the dead woman and the lake had conspired to avenge the killing. Even in death, Hallie still had something to say.

After the trial, the story lived on, becoming lore and legend. Visitors to the Olympic Peninsula still ask local librarians and Olympic National Park officials for more details about the Lady of the Lake. Children, especially, are fascinated by the tale of the murdered woman who "turned to soap." Researchers still pore through newspaper accounts, now brittle with age.

Hallie Illingworth achieved notoriety as the Lady of the Lake that she never came close to attaining when she was alive. Hers was a hardscrabble background; she lived through hard times. Repeatedly, she moved west, searching for a better life.

An early photograph of
Hallie Latham Illingworth.

She chased her dreams across the plains and the mountains, and finally to the edge of the continent. It proved to be her undoing.

The Early Years

Hallie Brooks Latham was born January 8, 1901, in Greenville, Kentucky, a farm town of about 1,000 people, located about 135 miles southwest of Louisville. She was the fifth child of Finis Marion and Mary Susan "Bunnie" Latham, a hard-working farm couple who made a living raising corn and tobacco.

Tobacco was the cash crop in those days, when farmers drove their mules and wagons into town and hitched them along Main Street. The Greenville townsfolk were proud of their tidy community, with its tree-lined streets, its stately brick county courthouse and a bustling downtown that served as a trading center and gathering point for county residents.

When Hallie was a toddler, it was not unusual to see Victorian-era women strolling on Main Street, the hems of their long, heavy dresses trailing in the road. Horse-drawn carriages still moved through town, often stopping at the LaMeade Hotel, a three-story showplace in the heart of downtown. Occasionally, Civil War veterans hobbled on canes into town to swap stories with other old-timers about battles fought not so long before.

The Lathams worked a farm about three miles south of Greenville, on what is now State Highway 181. One of

Hallie's chores was to take care of her little brothers and sisters as they arrived — thirteen in all — by 1920. Hallie grew especially close to her younger sisters, Cammie Bruce, Anna Margaret, Lois Christine and Laura Burke.

Thomas Brizendine archives, Greenville, Kentucky

Townsfolk in Greenville, Kentucky, were proud of their community, a trading center and gathering point for county residents.

Hallie's formal schooling ended in the eighth grade. Hard times hit the family, and about 1917, Finis Marion and Bunnie decided to pull up stakes and join their two oldest sons in the Dakotas. Scores of homesteaders and landseekers before them had piled their belongings into wagons and trucks and left Kentucky with high hopes for a better life. So Finis Marion and Bunnie gathered up Hallie and the rest of their brood. They headed west.

The Lathams farmed in a succession of small towns in the southeast corner of South Dakota, then moved to Faulkton, a rural community on the central prairie. Though the family made a living, there were plenty of mouths to feed. Life was not easy.

Hallie wanted more. She was changing from a girl to a young woman, and her world was changing just as much as she. More and more, farmers saw automobiles charging across the countryside. Life was going faster. The Victorian era was fading.

But marriage was still the dream for teenage girls. On September 26, 1919, in Mitchell, South Dakota, 18-year-old Hallie married Floyd James Spraker, a likable, down-to-earth auto mechanic who had served in World War I. Floyd's family had a stake in the future — his father ran an auto agency in Wagner, South Dakota. This was a step up for Hallie. The newly-weds lived for a time with Floyd's parents in Wagner, then settled near Hallie's parents in Faulkton.

For almost ten years, Hallie and Floyd built a life together. They had a daughter, Doris Marie, and lived in a one-story bungalow with a big porch in front and another out back. Floyd worked as a salesman, and, for a time, Hallie stayed home. She grew a garden. Often when company came to dinner, she picked green beans, carrots and other vegetables from her garden, fixed a pot roast and whipped up a delicious home-cooked meal topped off with her specialty — homemade lemon-chiffon pie.

The 1920s were good to her. Vivacious, with thick, auburn hair, Hallie had an outgoing personality and made friends easily. It was a free-wheeling time. The Roaring 20s, with its prohibition and bootleg liquor, made lawbreakers of a generation of young people, and chances are Hallie and Floyd were among them. It is known that Floyd enjoyed a drink, and it is likely Hallie did too.

But her early years of struggle and uprootedness had taken their toll on her. She grew discontented. Strong-willed and independent, driven by a need for security, Hallie wanted a better life for herself. She worked as a beauty operator and a waitress. She took up poultry farming.

Still, family members were surprised when Hallie and Floyd's marriage broke up in the late 1920s. The breakup could not have come at a worse time. On October 29, 1929, the stock market crashed. The Great Depression followed. Then droughts in 1931 and 1932 in South Dakota devastated crops.

But Hallie was upbeat and optimistic about the future. She believed that good times were coming, and life would be better tomorrow.

And it was. Hallie was working as a waitress in Gettysburg, South Dakota, when she met Donald B. Strickland, a young man who was in the restaurant business. Though at 31, Hallie was seven years older than Donald, she was not put off by the age difference. She shaved five years off her age on the marriage license, described herself as a widow, and married Donald on August 8, 1932, in Elk Point, South Dakota.

The Depression worsened in farm country. Grain prices fell so low that farmers complained they couldn't make a living. Soon, the newlyweds decided to flee the prairie. They packed up their belongings. They headed west.

Seattle

Hallie and Donald moved to Seattle, which was bursting at the seams with about 370,000 people. Like other parts of the country, Seattle had its share of the homeless and unemployed, but there was hope in the air — a perfect climate for Hallie's optimism.

Museum of History & Industry

An area of shacks south of the Smith Tower in Seattle became known as Hooverville during the Great Depression.

Hundreds of young people were finding work in various federal public works programs in the Northwest through the Civilian Conservation Corps. As time went on, they planted trees, put up bridges, built ranger stations; they worked as historians and artists. More jobs opened up in 1933, when ground was broken in eastern Washington for Grand Coulee Dam. Thousands of men poured into the state hoping to find work on the big government project.

Hallie and Donald worked hard to make ends meet. They ran a restaurant at the corner of Broadway and East Pine Street in Seattle, across from Edison Technical School. They probably lived above the restaurant, and Hallie's daughter, Doris, may have lived with them.

But only a short year after it began, Hallie and Donald's marriage began to crumble. The two separated, and Hallie's life was in upheaval again. Like she had so many times before, Hallie turned her eyes westward.

West of Seattle lay the promise of a better life, another chance. The Olympic Peninsula was a place to start over. Remote, and in some places, barely accessible, it was bordered by the Strait of Juan de Fuca and Canada to the north and the Pacific Ocean to the west. It was the farthest northwest a person could go and still be in the United States.

Unwilling to admit defeat despite her second failed marriage, Hallie made up her mind. She headed west once more to the end of the line — the Olympic Peninsula.

It was a fateful decision.

The Olympic Peninsula

Hallie took a job as a waitress at the Lake Crescent Tavern, a rustic lodge with rental cabins on the southern shore of Lake Crescent. The lodge offered a sweeping view of the lake, a crescent-shaped jewel in the heart of the Olympic Mountains. Surrounding the lake were forests of huge old-growth cedar trees, Douglas fir, and hemlock that grew tall and thick as far as the eye could see.

Olympic National Park/Photo reproduction by Ross Hamilton

The Lake Crescent Tavern looked like this in the mid-1930s when Hallie worked there as a waitress. The tavern now is known as the Lake Crescent Lodge.

For years, vacationers had boarded ferries north of Seattle, crossed Puget Sound, then settled into their Model

T's and Packard roadsters and made their way to one of the resorts on the shores of the lake. There, weary city folk enjoyed the scenery, fished for trout, hiked in the woods and ate home-cooked meals. It was a relaxed life.

One day in late 1934 or early 1935, Hallie was waiting on tables at the tavern when in came a tall, husky beer truck driver, Montgomery "Monty" J. Illingworth. Monty was born in 1908 in Ruskin, Nebraska, and had lived in Long Beach, California, before moving to the Olympic Peninsula. Like Hallie, Monty had been married and divorced. He also had a daughter, Patricia, and an ex-wife, Esther, who was on his trail for his failure to pay child support.

Monty was a ladies' man — nice looking, personable and friendly. He was also promiscuous, according to some. As a beer truck driver, Monty made daily rounds of taverns and stores on the Peninsula, where he chatted with bartenders and sold beer and other beverages. He liked to drink and party, and so did Hallie. Not surprisingly, the two hit it off.

Hallie was in her mid-30s, five years older than Monty, and though she was still beautiful, she was self-conscious about the age difference. She never told Monty that she wore a partial dental plate, made especially for her by a South Dakota dentist. She had bunions on her feet. She smoked.

Both of them drank. Frequently, they fought. Once, in

1936, Hallie and Monty were drinking at the Maple Grove Tavern, a resort area not far from Lake Crescent, when a fight broke out between Hallie and a woman sitting at the bar. Hallie, convinced that the other woman was eyeing Monty, walked over and knocked the woman off a barstool in a fit of jealous rage.

But the fights didn't cool Hallie and Monty's attraction for each other.

On June 16, 1936, Hallie and Monty were married by a justice of the peace in Seattle. The newlyweds returned to the Olympic Peninsula and set up housekeeping in the downstairs rooms of a wood-frame house in Port Angeles, a town of about 10,000. Monty drove his beer truck, and Hallie continued to work as a waitress. But her life was beginning to take a dangerous course.

Hallie and Monty's relationship grew increasingly violent. Five months into their marriage, the couple got into a pre-dawn fight that was so fierce the police were called to break it up. Weeks later, Hallie and Monty were at it again. Their landlady heard the shouts. "Oh Monty, don't," Hallie cried.

Hallie showed up for work with bruises on her face and arms. Sometimes she had black eyes. On occasion, Monty punched Hallie and knocked her down in front of her friends and co-workers.

Why Hallie stayed with her husband is a mystery,

though it's clear Monty had a powerful nature that women found compelling. He may have tapped into Hallie's primitive side, and she responded to his caveman brutishness. It may be that after so many years of struggle and hard work, Hallie was vulnerable and felt she needed someone to take care of her. Whatever the reason, Hallie stuck with her husband and fought back, even though she was no match for him. Monty was nearly a foot taller than his wife and weighed more than 200 pounds.

Monty and Hallie existed on the edge. They lived from paycheck to paycheck and spent money on parties and alcohol. They ran with a fast crowd that liked to party at each other's houses, or get drunk in bars along Front Street in Port Angeles.

Often the drinking led to fights between the two. Once Monty choked Hallie so hard, she was unable to swallow, and a friend had to feed her. Another time, Monty punched Hallie in the face, and she bit Monty on his arm. "I should have killed her," Monty told a hotelkeeper.

Instead, he played on her vulnerabilities, her jealousies. His behavior often made her furious.

Once, Hallie followed Monty to a nearby hot springs and raised hell when she found a woman in the cab of Monty's truck. Another time, Hallie spotted Monty's car in front of a notorious Port Angeles whorehouse and stormed inside looking for him. Monty threatened to choke her.

At times, Hallie vowed to leave her husband, and other times Monty swore he was going to walk out. But in June 1937, the couple marked one year of marriage, and carved out some stability in their star-crossed relationship. They lived in an apartment on a steep bluff in Port Angeles that overlooked the Strait of Juan de Fuca. On clear days it was possible to look across the strait and see the lights of Victoria and Vancouver Island. On the best of days, Mount Baker came into view in the distance.

Three months after Hallie and Monty's one-year anniversary, President Franklin Roosevelt visited the Olympic Peninsula to get a firsthand look at the 634,000 acres proposed for Olympic National Park. Throngs of people welcomed the president on September 30, 1937, in Port Angeles as his motorcade passed by the Clallam County Courthouse. That night Roosevelt stayed at Lake Crescent Tavern.

As the holiday season approached, Hallie and Monty made plans to have dinner with friends at Lake Crescent on Christmas Day.

Hallie's Disappearance

A cold wave began to sweep across the Peninsula on December 21, 1937. Strong winds blew. Despite predictions of snow, Monty announced that he was going to a beer bust that night at Fort Worden, a military base west of Seattle. He and Hallie fought. "She got sore about that," Monty said later.

With four days to Christmas, stores and the post office in Port Angeles stayed open late. All along First Street, stores were decorated for holiday shoppers. Hallie dashed off a Christmas card to her sister in Montana. The card depicted the shepherds' search for the lost lamb.

Sometime that day, Hallie put on rayon panties and a reinforced bra. She pulled a pair of silk stockings over her feet, slid her garters on, and rolled the stockings and garters up above her knees. She slipped on a green wool dress that Monty had given her the money to buy, cinched a covered-belt around her small waist and went out the door.

By nightfall, Hallie was ready to go out on the town. Braving the wind, she made her way to the Annex Hotel, a popular waterfront-area hangout for her and her friends. She opened the hotel door and climbed the steps to the hotel lobby.

A party was going on.

Hallie must have recognized several people who were regulars at the hotel; in fact, she and Monty sometimes kept a room there. Rooms were small, but guests and visitors could look out the windows and see the city and the Strait of Juan de Fuca, including a bird's-eye view of Ediz Hook, a two-mile-long spit that jutted into the waterway separating the United States and Canada. Next door, at the Pavilion Rink, youthful revelers roller-skated across the wood floors at a party sponsored by the Junior Chamber of Commerce.

Hallie was in a party mood and had a drink. Then another. Before long, she picked a fight with a woman, and the hotel housekeeper called the police. When the police arrived, Hallie and the woman promised to be quiet. But about midnight, Hallie and her friends left the hotel and drove to the home of one of the partygoers.

Hallie had still more drinks. Finally, about 2 a.m., she decided to leave. She and a friend left the party and walked to Hallie's car. Hallie opened the door and got behind the wheel. She started the car and pulled away, clipping a partygoer with the car door. At some point, her passenger got out of the car and Hallie drove alone down the deserted streets of Port Angeles.

Her friends never saw her again.

Wind whipped the trees as Monty headed home at about 2 a.m. from Fort Worden. Roaring in from the north, the wind kicked up waves in the Strait of Juan de Fuca. Huge swells lifted and dropped logs corralled in the harbor. Logs broke free and crashed against pilings. Snow began to fall in the foothills of the Olympics as Hallie and Monty made their separate ways home.

Lake Crescent

The sandy bottom of Lake Crescent was cold and dark. Fish rarely ventured into the deathly gloom. Indeed, the cold alone drove most living things away.

Earthquakes and a subsequent rock slide hundreds of years before had dammed a stream and helped create Lake Crescent. But the S'Klallam Tribe tells a richer story. Legend says that Lake Crescent came into being when Mount Storm King, a nearby peak, hurled a giant boulder into the glacial valley to stop two tribes from fighting each other. All the warriors were killed, and in their places emerged a peaceful lake about 12 miles long and more than 600 feet deep at its western end.

It was in this pristine place that someone tried to conceal a murder. A large bundle, wrapped with blankets and tied with rope, was slipped beneath the lake's surface. Apparently weighted, the bundle sank, coming to rest on the sandy bottom, at a spot probably 300 feet deep. The lake's bottom was as dark and still as a crypt.

The bundle lay in the darkness as the season above turned from winter to spring. Snowmelt from the Olympic Mountains trickled into creeks and streams that fed the lake. With the coming of spring, snowmelt gushed into Barnes Creek, Smith Creek and a handful of other waterways and poured into Lake Crescent.

Months passed, a year, then another year, and still the bundle lay on the dark, sandy bottom. Fresh water spilled into the lake, cycling the old water, turning it over and over and washing the bundle deep below.

As time wore on, the bundle began to fray and the ropes began to rot. Sometimes wood, sometimes gravel bumped against the bundle, weakening the blankets and the rope. More time passed and a chemical change occurred. The bundle became lighter, more buoyant.

One summer day, the bundle broke free. It rose toward the light and bobbed to the surface.

A Body is Discovered

The bundle retrieved by fishermen on July 6, 1940, turned out to be the body of a woman. The body was taken to a woodshed next to a mortuary in Port Angeles. Investigators were called in to help identify the dead woman and to find out the cause of death. It was clear the woman had been murdered.

North Olympic Library System/Photo reproduction by Ed Hosselkus

The body of an unidentified woman lies in a woodshed in Port Angeles.

Twenty-six-year-old Harlan McNutt had just finished his first year of medical school at George Washington University in Washington, D.C. He was on summer break in Port Angeles when he was asked to examine the body. As a medical student he had seen dead bodies and even dissected a few, but he had never seen anything quite like this.

The woman lay on coverings that had been spread on the planked floor. She was hog-tied. Her legs, arms, thighs and waist were bound with rope. She wore a belted, green wool dress and stockings with garters rolled above the knee. Shreds of blanket hung from her body.

"Let's get this rope undone," ordered Charlie Kemp, the sheriff of Clallam County, where the murdered woman was found.

McNutt kneeled down by the body and looked closely at the woman for the first time. The upper part of her face, her upper lip and nose were gone. Because her hands had been exposed, the tips of the fingers were gone. There was no way to get any fingerprints, and no way to tell what the woman looked like.

Something else was very unusual about the body. The flesh was soft. It broke easily. The dead woman's flesh had turned to something like Ivory Soap, McNutt said later, describing a condition known as "saponification." The soap-like condition resulted from the minerals in the lake interacting with the fats in the woman's body. The lake's near-freezing temperatures had virtually refrigerated the body for a long time.

A visual inspection of the body and a subsequent autopsy showed that the woman met a violent death. Her neck was bruised and discolored, and her chest showed evidence of extensive hemorrhage. She had been beaten and strangled.

A medical report noted bunions on her feet and an especially large bunion on her right toe. She was big-breasted and had brown or auburn-colored hair. But one clue emerged that ultimately turned the case around.

McNutt leaned over and tried to open her mouth. It was difficult. Her face was stiff and McNutt didn't want to disfigure the body.

Sheriff Kemp, impatient, said, "I'll get her goddamn mouth open." He pried open the woman's mouth.

The whole jaw came off, McNutt recalled.

But the grisly accident led to a startling discovery. The dead woman wore a distinctive gold upper dental plate.

It proved to be the clue that led to her killer.

The Hunt for the Killer

Sheriff Kemp sent out a circular to dentists with an illustration of the partial plate and offered a $100 reward to anyone who could identify its owner. More than a year passed before Dr. Albert J. McDowell, an elderly South Dakota dentist, identified the gold partial dental plate as one he had made for Hallie Latham Spraker in October 1926, when she lived in Faulkton.

McDowell's identification came on the heels of rumors that had already been circulating since Hallie's disappearance. A Port Angeles union official had reported the waitress missing. Hallie's close-knit family insisted that if Hallie were alive she would write letters or stay in touch in some way.

Soon, investigators were looking for Monty Illingworth, who was known to have abused his wife and was a logical suspect. He was traced to Long Beach, California, where he was working as a bus driver and living with Elinore Pearson, the attractive, blond daughter of a well-to-do Port Angeles lumberman.

Meanwhile, investigators followed up on reports that Hallie was alive. Max Church, the Clallam County prosecuting attorney, sent off telegrams to Alaska trying to track down rumors — most likely advanced by Monty — that Hallie was living there. Detective Hollis B. Fultz, a consulting criminologist with the Washington State Attorney General's office, drove from the state capital in Olympia to Bremerton on the trail of a naval officer reported to be the man Hallie ran off with.

But none of the leads turned up Hallie. Prosecutor Church and Detective Fultz closed in on Monty.

On October 26, 1941, Monty was arrested by Los Angeles sheriff's deputies and taken into custody in Los Angeles. That same day, Prosecutor Church caught a Southern Pacific train in San Francisco and headed to Los Angeles to meet with Detective Fultz.

The country was on the brink of war. In Russia, Soviet troops were stubbornly resisting Nazi advances outside Moscow, and Japan was stepping up production of war ships. Military leaders in Tokyo were devising strategies to cripple America's military operations in Hawaii. Pearl Harbor was six weeks away.

In Los Angeles, October 27 was a dreary day with low clouds and occasional showers. When Prosecutor Church arrived at Union Station in Los Angeles, he tipped the porter and caught a cab into town.

That night, Church joined Detective Fultz and Arthur Seth, a Los Angeles County sheriff's deputy, and Monty in Room 238 of the Los Angeles County Hall of Justice. It was time to talk to Monty.

Monty told the investigators that Hallie had deserted him. "I was home and she came home. She had been drinking. I left. When I came home, she was gone. She took her stuff and left." It was unclear when Monty last saw his wife.

The investigators knew that Monty had several versions of this story. Fultz confronted Monty. "How do you account for the fact that no person has seen her since she was living with you . . . until we found her in the lake, wrapped in blankets?"

"Well, it is as much a mystery to me as it is to you," said Monty.

"I think you killed Hallie," said Fultz, who had a reputation as a bulldog detective. "But I don't think you did it on purpose. You would beat her up. You would fight all the while. You came home that morning and she was there. She was mad, and before you were through with Hallie, she was dead. You didn't intend to do it. I know that just as well as I am standing on my two feet talking to you."

The investigators pressed on, suspicious of Monty's relationship with Elinore Pearson. Hallie had known Pearson; in fact Pearson had lived with Hallie's sister, Lois. Yet, only days after Hallie's fateful night, Monty took up with Pearson.

"I was up to her house quite a bit," Monty said. "We

were friendly. You know what I mean?"

"You were intimate, were you not?" Church asked.

"Yes," said Monty.

The investigators were incredulous. Within a month or so of Hallie's disappearance, Monty was living openly in Port Angeles with Pearson. How could he live with another woman if he believed that Hallie, a notoriously jealous woman, was still alive?

"Hallie was just the kind of woman who wouldn't allow anybody to poach around her preserves," Church argued.

"Yes, she was jealous," said Monty. "There is no doubt of that."

When Monty was shown a photo of the body of the murdered woman, he claimed the photo wasn't necessarily Hallie. "How do you know that is her?" Monty asked.

"We have identified her by the teeth," Fultz said. "We have found the dentist who made the teeth. We have her hair and her size."

"You remember her right foot?" asked Fultz. "You remember anything about the trouble she used to have getting shoes?"

"Yes," said Monty.

"She had a great big bunion on her right toe?"

"Yes," said Monty.

"All right, then, that is there," said Fultz. "Do you remember how she wore her socks? I will tell you. She always wore elastic garters right above the knee. Those were there too. Do you remember the kind of brassiere?" Fultz continued. Because Hallie was big breasted, her brassieres were reinforced. The victim was wearing a reinforced brassiere.

"Well, if it is her, why would I do it?" Monty asked.

"Just simply for what I told you," Fultz answered. "I have told you why. You did it. I have told you exactly why you did it, Monty."

It was nearly midnight before the investigators finished taking Monty's statement.

Monty swore he didn't kill Hallie and insisted she was still alive when he last saw her. It was a defense Monty and his attorney would use when his trial for first-degree murder commenced in Port Angeles four months later.

The Trial

S pectators began arriving early on February 24, 1942, at the red-brick Clallam County Courthouse in Port Angeles, as Monty Illingworth went on trial for Hallie's murder.

North Olympic Library System/Photo reproduction by Ross Hamilton

The murder trial was held in the Clallam County Courthouse in Port Angeles, shown here in an undated photograph.

The country was at war, but news of the trial often over-shadowed war news. It was a lurid tale of murder, abuse, drinking, betrayal, and an escape from a watery grave.

Homemakers, teenagers and curiosity seekers converged on the courtroom and, at times during the nine-day trial, spilled out into the halls. A section of the gallery in the courtroom was roped off for witnesses and other trial participants. Onlookers strained to catch a glimpse of Elinore Pearson, the "other woman," and Monty's devoted mother, Flossie Illingworth. As the trial progressed, some people carried lunches. Some brought knitting.

North Olympic Library System/Photo reproduction by Ed Hosselkus

Monty Illingworth is flanked by his mother, Flossie Illingworth, left, and his girlfriend, Elinore Pearson.

The jurors were a varied group — farmers, a bookkeeper, a millworker, a druggist, a homemaker, a businessman. They listened as the two sides made their cases. Monty's fate depended upon whether jurors believed the murdered woman was Hallie, or whether the jury believed Hallie was alive.

North Olympic Library System/Photo reproduction by Ross Hamilton

Jurors pose for a photograph with the jury matron and bailiff.

Monty's attorney, Joseph Johnston, brought in witnesses who said they saw Hallie after 1937. He put experts on the stand who said that the body could not have been in Lake Crescent for 31 months. He grilled Dr. Albert McDowell, the South Dakota dentist.

But McDowell held his ground. The old dentist said he was positive that the dental plate found on the murdered woman belonged to Hallie.

Hallie's brother-in-law, James Johnson, identified the woman found in Lake Crescent as Hallie. One by one, family members and a friend of Hallie's walked up to the witness box, swore to tell the truth and sat down in the chair.

Was the underwear the kind Hallie wore?

It was, they said.

Was the hair sample taken from the murdered woman similar to Hallie's?

It was, they said.

Was the dead woman's dress similar to Hallie's?

It was, they said.

Each piece of evidence, each article of clothing so carefully preserved by the cold, clear lake strengthened the case that the murdered woman was Hallie.

Jesse Hudson Knapp, who once clerked at Montgomery Ward and sold Hallie a green wool dress, testified that Hallie had a small waist and often added an extra notch to her belts. The covered-belt was cinched tighter than normal on the murdered woman who lay for so long on the sandy bottom of Lake Crescent.

Harry Brooks, who ran a resort near Lake Crescent Tavern, said he loaned about 50 feet of rope to a beer truck driver. Experts compared remnants of the rope that Brooks still had with fibers from the rope used to hog-tie the murdered woman. The rope that had clung to the body in the depths of Lake Crescent matched the rope that Brooks had. The beer truck driver was Monty.

Monty Illingworth takes the witness stand.

When Monty took the stand, he swore Hallie left him the day after the two got home from drinking that December night. But a number of witnesses said otherwise, including a friend and co-worker of Monty's. Monty had told different stories to each person.

"I didn't kill anybody," Monty shouted in the crowded courtroom.

It took the jurors four hours to reach a verdict. On March 5, 1942, the jury found Monty guilty of second-degree murder. He was sentenced to life imprisonment at the Washington State Penitentiary in Walla Walla.

It was justice at long last for the murdered woman. A contemporary of Hallie's later observed that her murder was most likely not premeditated, that Hallie and Monty probably had a fight in their apartment on that cold winter night in 1937. The fight took a violent turn and Monty brutally beat and strangled Hallie to death. Though Monty tried to cover up the crime by disposing of his wife's body in Lake Crescent, the lake proved to be Hallie's ally. It was as though the dead woman and the lake conspired to avenge her murder. Hallie, in death, was able to tell the final episode of her restless life that ended too soon.

Epilogue

Monty Illingworth served nine years for second-degree murder and was paroled January 10, 1951. He died in Los Alamitos, California, on November 5, 1974.

Before Hallie's killer was brought to trial, family members moved her body from a pauper's grave in Port Angeles to a cemetery in Vancouver, Washington, a community on the Columbia River where other family members lived. Hallie was buried there on January 24, 1942. Her gravesite is unmarked.

Little is known about what happened to Hallie's first husband, Floyd J. Spraker, but the couple's daughter, Doris Marie, apparently took up residence in California. Donald B. Strickland, Hallie's second husband, served in the U.S. Army during World War II and fought in the Battle of the Bulge in 1944. He died February 19, 1985, in Custer, South Dakota.

Hallie's father and mother, Finis Marion and Bunnie, moved from Faulkton to Mellette, South Dakota, where they rented a farm for several years. They apparently moved back to Greenville for a time, but settled in Minneapolis, Minnesota, where Finis died January 2, 1951, and Bunnie died August 15, 1964.

Max Church, the prosecutor who put Monty behind bars, went on to become Superior Court judge for Clallam and Jefferson counties. He retired in 1963 and interestingly was succeeded by

Joseph Johnston, Monty's attorney. Church died of pneumonia at age 75 on a cruise ship, January 24, 1964.

Hollis B. Fultz, the bulldog detective who so aggressively interviewed Monty, was a prolific crime writer. He was the author of *Famous Northwest Manhunts,* published in 1955. In 1959, Fultz ran successfully for coroner in Thurston County, where Olympia, the Washington State capital is located. He was coroner for 16 years. Fultz died of a heart attack at age 87 on July 26, 1975, in Olympia.

Dr. Harlan McNutt, who as a young medical student examined Hallie's body after she was taken from Lake Crescent, retired to Port Angeles. He has often been asked to tell the story of the murdered woman he first saw lying on the floor of the woodshed more than half a century ago.

Acknowledgments

This is a true story. Grateful acknowledgment is made to the following for their help in my research: Clallam County Courthouse staff in Port Angeles, Dr. Harlan McNutt, Petrus "Pete" Pearson, Norman Brooks, all from Clallam County; Laura Burke Latham Dunbar, Florida; and Gayle Carver, Greenville, Kentucky.

My thanks to Joan Ducceschi of Port Angeles for reviewing and editing an early draft of the story. Thanks also to Roberta Sobotka of Corvallis, Oregon, who reviewed the final manuscript.

I appreciate photographers Ross Hamilton and Ed Hosselkus who provided the vintage photographs, and Rich Riski who took the color photo of Lake Crescent for our cover. I am grateful for the photograph archives at the North Olympic Library System, Olympic National Park and the Museum of History & Industry in Seattle.

Seattle graphics designer Jennifer O'Brien did a wonderful job designing our book cover. My thanks to her. Also, a special thanks to my partner, George Erb, for his unwavering support. Finally, I appreciate the *Peninsula Daily News* in Port Angeles and Publisher John Brewer for taking part in this project.

About the Author

Mavis Amundson lived on the Olympic Peninsula from 1987 to 1992. A journalist, she is the editor of the best-selling Peninsula book, *Sturdy Folk*, an oral history of the Olympic Peninsula. She lives in Seattle.